GEORGE BENJAMIN

Ringed by the Flat Horizon

for full orchestra

(1979-80)

FABER ff MUSIC

Ringed by the Flat Horizon was written for the Cambridge University Musical Society
and first performed by the CUMS orchestra conducted by Mark Elder on 5 March 1980

The first London performance was given by the BBC Symphony Orchestra
conducted by Mark Elder at a Henry Wood Promenade Concert at
the Royal Albert Hall on 25 August 1980

Ringed by the Flat Horizon is recorded by the BBC Symphony Orchestra
conducted by Mark Elder on Nimbus Records NI 5075 (CD only)

Duration: 20 minutes

© 1981, 1994 by Faber Music Ltd
First published in 1981 by Faber Music Ltd
This edition published in 1994 by Faber Music Ltd
3 Queen Square London WC1N 3AU
Music drawn by Peter Vinson
Photograph by Dr W P Winn
Printed in England by Hobbs the Printers, Southampton
All rights reserved

ISBN 0 571 51078 7

for Olivier Messiaen

Who are these hooded hordes swarming
Over endless plains, stumbling in cracked earth
Ringed by the flat horizon only
What is the city over the mountains
Cracks and reforms and bursts in the violet air

from *The Waste Land* by T.S. Eliot
Reprinted by permission of Faber and Faber Ltd

A dramatic photograph of a thunderstorm over the New Mexico desert and an extract from T.S. Eliot's *The Waste Land* provided the inspiration for this piece.

I wanted to portray an eerie tension as a landscape is overwhelmed by a vast storm. The work starts slowly and mysteriously, with a succession of three textures that recur throughout the structure – weird, soft, bell chords, a sustained semitone clash, and deep tremors in the lower registers of the orchestra which depict distant thunder. Piccolo solos surrounded by high violins follow, and fuller developments of the opening ideas, gradually transform the momentum to faster music.

Here a sonority of wind and muted trumpets, punctuated by wooden percussion, is juxtaposed with quieter, more lyrical cello solos. These build with increasing intensity, culminating in a massive climax, after which the music slowly descends to the bass register, subsiding in a solitary bass-drum roll.

There follows a sequence of dark, ominous chords for full orchestra (a sound completely new to the piece), interspersed with solo melodic lines over the deep tremors of the opening. For a moment the original semitone clash hovers motionless in the air; the thunder at last erupts in a violent explosion; and the work returns to a mood of unreal calm, ending as it began, with a soft bell chord.

ORCHESTRA

3 Flutes (2nd and 3rd doubling Piccolos)
2 Oboes
Cor Anglais
3 Clarinets in B♭ (2nd doubling E♭, 3rd doubling Bass)
2 Bassoons
Double Bassoon

4 Horns in F
Trumpet in D
2 Trumpets in B♭
3 Trombones
Tuba

Percussion *(5 players):*

1. 4 Timpani, Side drum, Sizzle (nailed) cymbal

2. Bass drum *(very large and deep)*, 5 Temple blocks, 5 Small bongos, Glass chimes, Whip, Small suspended cymbal

3. Glockenspiel, Tam-tam *(very large)*, 3 Suspended cymbals, Triangle Tubular bells *(shared with 5)*

4. Vibraphone, Xylophone, Large suspended cymbal

5. Tubular bells, Cymbals (pair), 5 Temple blocks *(shared with 2)* 5 Small bongos *(shared with 2)*

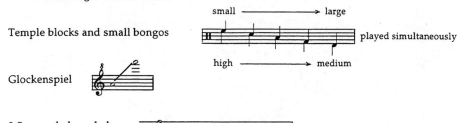

Temple blocks and small bongos — small ⟶ large / high ⟶ medium — played simultaneously

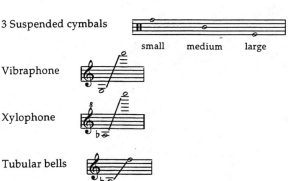

Glockenspiel

3 Suspended cymbals — small   medium   large

Vibraphone

Xylophone

Tubular bells

Celesta (4 octaves)
Piano
Harp

Strings *preferably 16.16.12.10.8 (basses 5-8 with low C string)*

Score in C

Orchestral parts available on hire

RINGED BY THE FLAT HORIZON

GEORGE BENJAMIN

Mysterious (Extremely slow; ♩=50) **Faster (♩=75)**

* It is vital that the pianist sustains the pedal throughout this — and later similar — passages.

N.B.: Those phrases marked between the following signs:⌐ ¬ must predominate above all other parts (and similarly in other passages).

Slower   a tempo   rall.

8

12

14

15

Pesante   a tempo [L]   accel. poco a poco............................

(accel.)

(accel.) - M Very fast (♩ = 126)

O Slower

23

Slower

T **a tempo**

U Moderately slow (♩= 54)

Very fast
(♩ = 126)

*   trills always of a semitone

40

* N.B. Tamtam: with hard Tubular Bell beater, and NOT normal soft mallet.

Very slow (♩ = 38)

48

rall......Slower   a tempo (♩ = 66)

GG

Solemn and dark (♩ = 55)

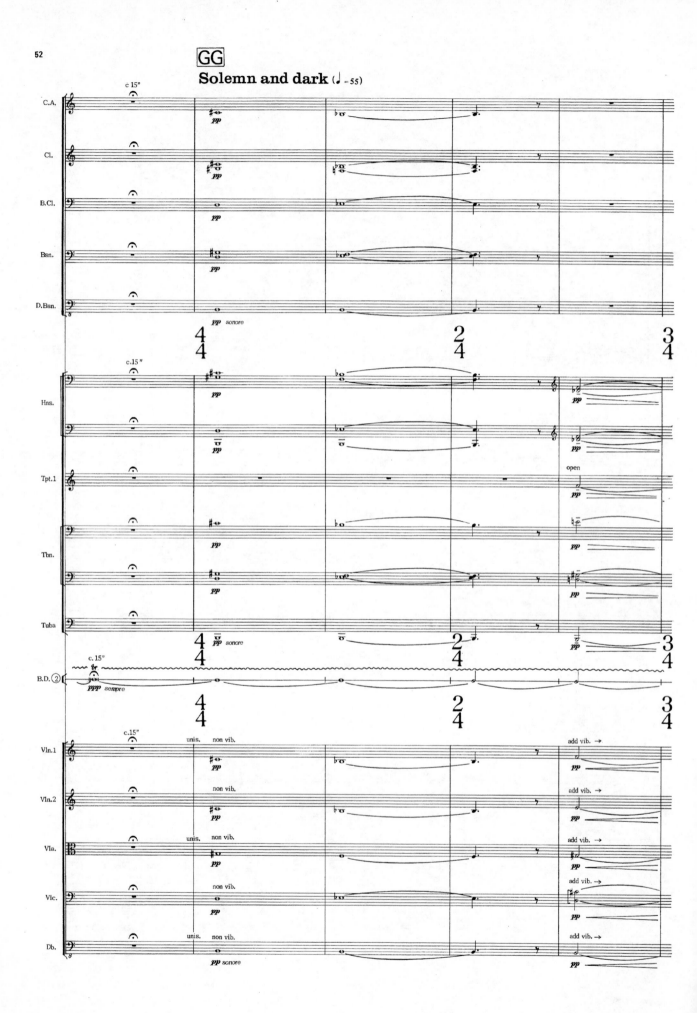

HH Slow (♩=66)

54

II

rall. - - - - - - - - - - - - **Solemn and dark** (♩=55)

Solemn and dark (♩ = 55)

NN
Slower ($\quad$ = 90)

rall. molto

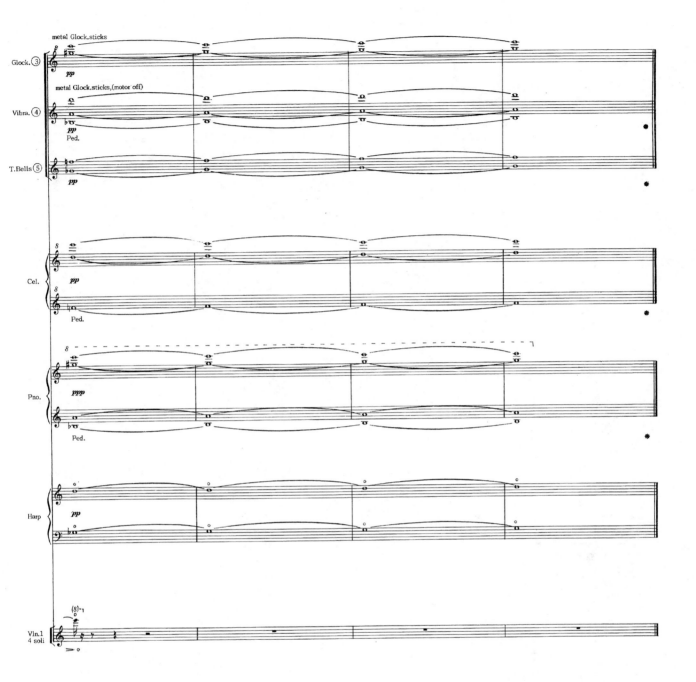